VERMONT
WITHDRAWN ONTPELIE

W9-BLF-317

MUST
THE WEST
DECLINE?

by

David Ormsby-Gore, Lord Harlech

WITHDRAWN

Columbia University Press 1966

NEW YORK & LONDON

Lord Harlech, then Sir David Ormsby-Gore,
served as British Ambassador to the United States
from 1961 to 1965.

Copyright © 1966 Columbia University Press
Library of Congress Catalog Card Number: 66-20135
Printed in the United States of America

910.03
H284m

Foreword

WITHDRAWN

TEN YEARS AGO the University was happy to accept a proposal by the family of the late William Radner, a graduate of Columbia College and the Columbia Law School, that a lecture series be established in the memory of this valiant young man, whose career in the public service had been terminated by his early and untimely death. Appropriately, these lectures were to deal with government and the public service.

In our day foreign and domestic affairs have become so interconnected that few questions of public policy can be considered seriously without including an analysis of both factors as they bear upon the ultimate process of statecraft, which is decision-making. Actually, in many instances foreign affairs largely determine the framework within which domestic decisions must be made. Tax policy, financial management, trade policy—all these and many others fall into this category.

Among the foreign questions which have a profound effect on our public policy at home, none is more fundamental than that of our posture *vis-à-vis* the Communist

19629

world, and this posture, in turn, will be influenced deci-
sively by the final decisions to be made concerning the
organization of the Atlantic Community. The remarkable economic recovery of Western Europe and the re-
surgence of strong nationalistic doctrines in some European countries have combined to create a situation which
has been detrimental to Western unity and beneficial to
those who wish to keep the West in a state of disorgani-
zation. Some observers view the present state of affairs as
inevitable; others believe that unity can be regained
through specific policy projects such as the hotly de-
bated MLF proposal; still others assert that no genuine
progress will be possible until the states of Western Europe have managed to create greater unity of action and
policy among themselves, a result which would provide
a basis for more effective partnership with the massive
power position of the United States.

These are the questions to which Lord Harlech has
addressed himself in the 1965 Radner lectures. By virtue
of his own unquestioned scholarship and his long experience in the practice of diplomacy, he is admirably fitted
to deal expertly with these complex and perplexing matters, upon the solution of which the future of Western
civilization may so largely depend. Every reader will
find in his observations objectivity and wisdom, qualities
which were never more needed by statesmen on both
sides of the Atlantic. The University is grateful to him
for his willingness in the midst of a busy career to set
down for its audience and for the wider public his own

considered views on the steps which must be taken by the West if it is to preserve for the future those values upon which its civilization has been built.

GRAYSON KIRK

Columbia University
February, 1966

Contents

Must the West Decline?

ONE

Western Civilization—Its Failings

IT IS NOW a cliché to say that in this era of human history we live in "one world." But clichés often enshrine great truths; and many of the actions, and above all the attitudes, of peoples and governments today seem to derive from earlier times, when the connection between nations and societies in different parts of the globe was tenuous in the extreme. If we are to make sense of our present environment on earth and if we are to pursue wise policies, we must slough off these mental attitudes of a bygone age and think on a global scale. For these reasons the Western world owes Arnold Toynbee a great debt of gratitude for compelling us in his monumental *Study of History* to examine our society within the context of the whole panorama of human life. Toynbee, having set certain criteria for the identification of individual civilizations, comes to the conclusion that there have been a total of twenty-one, including our own Western civilization as it exists today. He has also attempted to show how there is a certain rhythm in the affairs of men which can account for the rise, the decline, and the fall of civilizations. One does not necessarily have to accept his diagnosis as being 100 percent accurate, but one is certainly aware of the simple fact that great civilizations have declined and have fallen.

What have been the main causes of such a decline and fall? They have been many and varied. So varied, in fact, that in order to contain them, any universal formulas become so broad as to be virtually meaningless and therefore valueless. Nevertheless, even if we avoid formulas, it is not hard to discern certain basic reasons for the decay or collapse of a civilization. Sometimes it has been due to the interior deterioration of the society. This was true of ancient Egypt and of the Hellenic civilization, which developed its final form in the Roman Empire. Sometimes it has been due to stagnation in the military arts; Persian numbers were no match for the Macedonian phalanx of Alexander, and the Incas were bound to go down before the Spaniards with their gunpowder, metal armor, and cavalry. Sometimes it has been due to exposure to a superior social system, and the most obvious examples of this are the collapse of primitive societies in Africa and the Antipodes once they came in contact with Western civilization stemming from Europe. More often it has been due to a combination of these and other factors.

We are living at a moment in history when what I have called Western civilization is being challenged on a global scale. It would therefore seem prudent to examine the present trends in our society and in the rest of the world to see whether there is evidence of decay in Western civilization which if not arrested could spell its doom. Are we luxuriating in the use of a wealthy inheritance while the foundations of our fortune are crumbling away? Have we lost that vital spark which sets alight the creative minds of individual men? Are we perhaps destined to go down before a more modern society better attuned to a world changed out of all recognition in the last one hundred years by science and technology?

If any of these things are even partly true, what can we and ought we to do about it?

Before we come to examine Western civilization with a critical eye, however, I feel I must define certain terms. This is necessary because it is possible to argue that Western civilization in one form or another is now predominant and indeed unchallenged throughout the entire world. This is because Marxism, though generally regarded as the main or even sole challenger to our civilization—as I, in fact, regard it—and now embraced by one-third of the human race, is entirely of Western origin. Karl Marx was, of course, a German who spent most of his life in Western Germany or London and more particularly in the reading room of the British Museum. He was therefore entirely the product of a West European environment, and it is a curiosity of history that a social system conceived in his brain and precisely tailored, he thought, to right the ills of Western industrial society has in practice been adopted principally by Eastern peoples living at the outset in overwhelmingly agrarian societies.

In spite of this paradox connected with the creation of modern Communism, I do not regard the social system developed by Lenin from Marx's original concept as a branch of Western civilization. In most important respects it is its antithesis. I therefore intend to use the words Western civilization to cover that system of society which owes something to the Hellenic civilization, a great deal to the Judeo-Christian religious tradition, much to the political philosophy developed by Western Europeans in their own countries or after being transplanted into the New World, and more recently something to the economic system that resulted from the Industrial Revolution. "In short," as Mr. Micawber would say, the kind of society which you and I live in; the kind that has been established and practiced, more or less successfully, in a great number of other countries who now constitute our friends and allies.

I suppose that the essence of such a society is the paramount importance which it attaches to the individual. It is based on a fundamental conviction that the State is made for man, not man for the State, and here we approach the key factor which distinguishes Western society from Communist society. We have tried to set up a system of government which has as its avowed purpose the provision of the maximum amount of freedom to individual men and women consistent with the enjoyment of such freedom by others. This is because of a belief in the supreme value of each individual, a belief which to my mind can have little meaning unless based upon a foundation of religious conviction. Needless to say, we have none of us achieved or even closely approached perfection in the creation of such a society, and there have, in fact, been lamentable examples within the Western world of nations who have taken a backward step into totalitarianism of varying degrees of villainy. Nazism in Germany is undoubtedly the worst example, and regrettably there still remain dictatorial systems of government which deny certain of the most elementary freedoms to their people.

In these cases, however, I think it would be fair to say that even within the ruling minority there is held a concept of the ideal human society which agrees broadly with the one I have outlined. That is to say, they regard the present restrictions as temporary measures required to prevent anarchy and to prepare for the time when a wider measure of democracy can safely be indulged in. But I do not want these references to these glaring examples of a failure to live up to the principles of Western civilization to blur the image of a form of society which is quite distinctive and which the vast majority of people in the United States and in Great Britain hold most dear. We are talking here of that whole complex made up of democratic government, the rule of law, a judiciary independent of the executive, equality before the law, freedom of speech, freedom of worship, and freedom of association, all of which we often take for granted but for which our forefathers have struggled and died over the centuries.

How has the civilization based on these concepts fared in the first half of the twentieth century and how well is it meeting the challenge of competing societies today? If we are to be frank with ourselves, we have to admit that it made a well-nigh disastrous start to this century. Within a single generation it indulged in two titanic wars which led to death and destruction on a scale that makes Genghis Khan or Attila look like amateurs in vandalism. Because of this mad and abominable eruption at the heart of the Western world, millions of its people were impoverished, as were others who had no part in the original quarrel but were nevertheless drawn into the vortex. It is in no way surprising that during and after World War I many thoughful humans began demanding a complete break with the past. If a system of conducting our affairs could bring about such universal suffering and misery, then it needed radical change. Without World War I it is most unlikely that Communism would ever have been riveted on the long-suffering Russian people. Without the bleak aftermath of that war those malignant growths Nazism and Fascism would not have struck root in Europe. Without World War II it is most probable that Communism would not have spread to Eastern Europe and to China.

Who or what was responsible for these twin catastrophes? To account for the first it is, of course, easy enough to point to the arrogance and chauvinism of Germany, to the monumental ineptitude and negligence of Austria, to the stupidity and incompetence of Russia, and to British and French inactivity until it was too late to save the situation. Then in 1939 it is easy enough to point an accusatory finger at Nazi Germany with Fascist Italy and Japan as accessories in the crime. And no doubt we were all guilty, if not of sins of commission, certainly of sins of omission, with Britain and America included. But can we not discern a more general basic cause? I think we can, and I believe it to be an exaggerated admiration and an altogether excessive reverence for the nation-state.

Now without question the nation-state had at a recent period in our history brought us many benefits and served a most useful purpose. Submerging parochial interests in the general national interest formed a much more efficient unit which enabled far more to be accomplished to the advantage of all citizens in the state. Without a measure of patriotism, individual sacrifices for the good of the community as a whole will not be forthcoming. But as a result of the industrial and scientific revolution of the nineteenth century the sovereign nation-state was rapidly becoming an anachronism. The nation still had an indispensable part to play in the scheme of things, but it was no longer complete and sufficient in itself, nor could it act solely in its own self-interest and ignore the interests of others without dire consequences and eventually intolerable friction.

It was because Karl Marx believed that individual nations under capitalism would behave in this way that he promulgated the doctrine of inevitable conflict between them, leading in the end to the triumph of Communism. As he saw it, we in the Western world could find no solution to our internal contradictions arising out of selfish nationalism, with the result that we would feel bound to resort to war. We very nearly proved him right, and if we are sufficiently foolish, we may yet do so. To the convinced Communist the outbreak of the two great wars in this century seemed to bear out with remarkable precision the predictions of the founding father, Karl Marx.

We can see, therefore, that our Western civilization has been living through a period of supreme crisis. If we failed to find a system of society in which the interests of all the nations that comprised it were made paramount over the interests of each individual nation, then there would be every likelihood of a decline and final collapse.

In this connection it has often seemed to me that we should from time to time try to look at our much vaunted civilization through the eyes of the new nations of Asia and Africa. Some of us tend to be surprised that they do not always seem to share our own admiration for the West's contribution to progress and political enlightenment in the world. But what are they to make of the West's conduct of its affairs in the first half of this century? They observe that the most violent and destructive wars in history broke out at the heart of Western civilization, and although they had had no part in the original quarrel, they too had to suffer as a result of it. To them also the Cold War seems to have the appearance of an extension of the conflict which officially ended in 1945. To many it seems that it is not their quarrel, but they are acutely conscious that if it gets out of control and ends in a hot war, they again will suffer. In this respect Western civilization is still very much on trial, and it is too early yet to say with confidence that we have learnt from our mistakes and have so modified our internal organization that it cannot again break down.

I have spoken so far mainly of the political record in the first half of this century, and I now turn to the economic and social items in the ledger. In all honesty, one is bound to admit that for the first forty years the record in this field is not much better. It seemed that the free-enterprise system which had grown out of the Industrial Revolution was bound to produce violent swings from boom to slump, and it was particularly disturbing that the intensity of these swings appeared to be increasing. By 1930 the whole economic system was on the verge of collapse, and the major industrial countries were in the worst plight of all. In the United States the catastrophic fall in stock values on Wall Street was followed by bank failures, stagnation in industry, and the misery of 10 million unemployed. In Britain we had the same stagnation and, in proportion to our population, a similar level of unemployment, 3 million being out of work. In Germany the situation was utterly disastrous; the middle class had already been destroyed by runaway inflation, and now the slump had produced a higher rate of unemployment than was suffered in either the United States or Britain. These were the appalling conditions in which the German people turned in desperation to Nazism, with dreadful consequences for the whole world.

It is not surprising that under these circumstances the Marxist analysis of the crisis gained popularity, particularly in Western Europe. Indeed, any intelligent person was bound to feel that there must be a better way of conducting our affairs. If it was not necessary to change our economic machine for a totally new model, as the Marxists suggested, at the very least the machine required drastic modifications. Even when the worst was over, by the mid-1930s there had been very little expansion in production in the industrialized countries of the West as compared with pre-slump levels, and the reported rates of growth in the Soviet Union were alarming to some and in the minds of others clear evidence of a superior economic system. It is, of course, true that production figures for the Soviet Union were manipulated and exaggerated for propaganda purposes, as they still are to some extent, but even the correct figures would have shown a faster and steadier rate of industrial expansion than we were experiencing in the West. State direction to the degree practiced by National Socialism in Germany was also showing a better industrial performance than the free-enterprise systems of the democracies.

If then we were to draw up a balance sheet at, say, the year 1939 or 1940, Western civilization would present a melancholy picture bordering on the calamitous. Through a combination of extreme nationalism and incompetent economic management, it had produced in the previous generation but little advance in living standards, great social evils of which mass unemployment was the most notable, and finally a second war, breaking out in Europe but spreading rapidly to engulf the world. When I say it is a shocking story, I am making no moral judgment. Wicked men and wicked ideas were abroad in the world, but mistakes were made by good, upright, and dedicated men and women. But whether the mistakes were made with good intentions or with bad intentions, we ought at least to profit from them and make sure we do not once again tread the same path.

When peace came in 1945, I think a consciousness of our earlier failures was deeply implanted in the minds of all who had survived the holocaust and not least in the minds of those who had experienced overwhelming defeat and humiliation. We were all of us determined to make a new and a better start. A praiseworthy spirit of cooperation and good-neighborliness was apparent, and in this respect the lead that was given by the United States must remain an imperishable ornament to that nation's history. Toynbee, in commenting on the aftermath of the war, has said, "In the past it had been cus-

tomary for victorious powers not to give, but to take,
and there had been no departure from this evil custom in
the policy of the Soviet Union. The Marshall Plan set a
new standard for which there was no comparable historic precedent." The administration of the assistance
given to Europe under the Marshall Plan gave birth to
the Organization for European Economic Co-operation,
the OEEC, now expanded and renamed the Organization for Economic Co-operation and Development
(OECD). But even before this, joint efforts had been
made to establish a satisfactory system to maintain or-
derly exchange arrangements through the International
Monetary Fund and to regulate the conduct of international trade outside the Communist bloc through the
General Agreement on Tariffs and Trade. The International Bank for Reconstruction and Development was
established to do what its name implies and to promote
foreign investment.

These and other bodies have since 1945 operated in a
manner which has brought an infinitely greater measure
of stability into the international monetary field than
was experienced in the aftermath of World War I, and I
suggest that the most notable feature of these arrangements is that they circumscribe the sovereignty, in practice if not in law, of the nations participating in them.
Members of these organizations have undertaken to
abide by certain rules of behavior that are designed to
redound to the general good and that impede unilateral
action, which might benefit an individual country only

at the expense of its neighbors. We have thus avoided competitive exchange depreciations, and we have been steadily dismantling barriers to trade through a series of negotiated tariff reductions and the elimination of various practices stemming from a narrow nationalistic approach to trade problems.

But perhaps what has been of even greater significance than this improvement in the international field is the far more effective management of our internal financial policies. We have had recessions, it is true, but they have never approached the intensity of those between the wars, and they have been little more than pauses on a steadily rising curve of production. In the United States, unemployment has been contained at about 5 percent of the working population. In Britain, it has been generally less than 2 percent, and in other Western countries, such as Germany, as low as 1 percent. All in all, the last twenty years seem to have disproved the charge that a free-enterprise system must inevitably be accompanied by booms and slumps and periods of heavy unemployment. It would be difficult to exaggerate the importance of this development in meeting the challenge of Communist society. If we had relapsed into the prewar pattern, with its harmful repercussions in every corner of the globe, the attractions of Communism would have been increased immeasurably and the charms of Western society similarly diminished.

In the competition between the two systems as to which can achieve the fastest rate of growth in the national product, it would be hard, however, to reach a final conclusion. If we take the main champions of the rival systems, the United States and the Soviet Union, I think we would have to say that up until 1960 the Soviet rate of expansion, even after heavily discounting some of the published figures, was clearly more rapid than that of the United States. I remember Jules Moch saying to me that he feared that unless the Western democracies could generate capital investment on a scale closely corresponding to that in Communist countries, they would in the long run be doomed. But the comparative performance of the two economic systems is an immensely complicated matter, and, even leaving out of account the question of the quality of the goods manufactured and the extent to which they meet the real needs and desires of the consumers, there is the problem of comparing two economies at very different stages in their development, the American economy being some stages ahead of the Russian economy. In Russia, for instance, during the 1950s there was still a vast pool of underemployed agricultural labor to be tapped for industry. This labor supply was not available to anything like the same extent in the United States and scarcely existed at all in Britain. It was noticeable, however, that in other free-enterprise economies, such as West Germany, Italy, and Japan, which like Russia were rebuilding from a low level of activity resulting from the war, rates of increase in the national product equaled or even exceeded the performance of the Soviet Union.

Then from 1960 onward we have seen new trends developing. The American economy has forged ahead with an unbroken period of expansion which at times has achieved a rate of 6 percent a year. At about the same time, the rate of increase in the Soviet Union began to falter, and in 1962 it may have been no more than 3 or 4 percent. All this is vastly encouraging and gives one every justification for saying that the conduct of our economic affairs both national and international within Western society has been very much more satisfactory since 1945 than during the previous forty years. There are nevertheless some dark clouds on the horizon which I shall come to a little later.

First, however, I want to examine how well we have been doing on the political front. Here again, we have made a much more promising start than after 1918. One has only to compare the state of affairs in the world twenty years after World War I with the state of affairs today, twenty years after World War II, for the improvement to be self-evident. In the first two years it is true that not much in the way of political cooperation was achieved. Great and, as it turned out, exaggerated hopes were placed in the United Nations Organization. It was overambitious to suppose that universal political cooperation would prove possible, particularly when two such fundamentally different societies as the Marxist-Leninist and the Western democracies were both represented in the organization. Quite soon it became obvious that, while not abandoning the objective of an effective

world organization, we would be wise to practice cooperation on a smaller scale between like-minded nations.
Fear was also as always a powerful stimulant, but even
without the very real threat from militant Communism,
there was a widespread desire in Western Europe to seek
for a unity which would insure that never again would
these immensely gifted nations try to solve their problems by tearing each other to pieces.

Monnet and Schumann in France, de Gaspari in Italy,
Spaak in Belgium, Stikker in the Netherlands, and later
on Adenauer in Germany, to name but a few of the
prime movers, held out to their respective peoples the vi-
sion of a united Europe resting on firm foundations and
capable once again of being an example and an inspira-
tion to the world. Gradually, and not without great
difficulty and prodigious effort, such a Europe began to
take shape, and it was supplemented by an integrated alliance, the North Altantic Treaty Organization, embrac-
ing all the like-minded nations of Europe and North
America. NATO differed from the old-fashioned military alliances of the past in that it accepted the necessity
for some merging of national sovereignty if the defense
of the West was to be placed upon a rational basis. All
the smaller and middle-sized powers, including such
powers as Britain and Germany, abandoned any attempt
to provide themselves with self-sufficient defense forces,
strategic and tactical, conventional and nuclear, on the
ground, in the air, and at sea. For each country to provide the means to resist a major assault alone would be to

with the problems of the modern world. We did seem, however, after an immense sacrifice of our own and other people's blood, sweat, and tears, to have learned some vital lessons that would enable us to set our course into a future full of hope and high promise. We must at all costs guard against the danger, which is a real one, of slipping back into the habits of mind that brought disaster upon the world twenty-five years ago. If through our own folly we again let loose the spirit of extreme nationalism, then we may yet find that we are living in the twilight of Western civilization.

TWO

Western Civilization—Its Strength

IT IS, of course, in the nature of human institutions that they are imperfect, and certainly our society is no exception to the rule. We can therefore measure its worth and its strength only in a relative way. We need to examine how Western civilization has met the formidable challenge presented to the whole human race by the industrial and scientific revolution of the past century and a half. We need also to examine how other societies have met the same challenge in order to see how ours has fared in comparison.

First, it is only being fair to ourselves and to our immediate ancestors to acknowledge that we have all had to wrestle with a change in our environment on this earth that has taken place at a speed and on a scale entirely unprecedented in human history. The men in my country who over the years developed a system of impartial justice and democratic government were without any doubt great and wise—as also were those very remarkable men who drew up the United States Constitution, but they lived in an environment whose main char-

acteristics had changed little for centuries. The distilled
wisdom and experience of generations was available to
them, and the conditions around them made the conclu-
sions arising from this knowledge more applicable and
pertinent to the problems they had to solve. People
could communicate with each other in person or by mes-
sage at the speed a horse could travel or a ship move with
sails to catch the wind, as had been the case for centuries.
Power to operate machines still came from animals,
humans, primitive waterpower, or the wind. Apart from
a few relatively small communities that specialized in the
entrepreneur trade, like Venice, all countries rested on
an agricultural base. In the military sphere, as recently as
the beginning of the last century Napoleon's armies
could move no faster than Julius Caesar or Alexander
had done more than 2,000 years earlier. Even that great
innovation, gunpowder, had reached Europe no less than
four centuries before. Up until the nineteenth century,
the economic, the political, and the military problems
that faced governments and their peoples remained
broadly similar to those that had faced them for over
two millenniums.

Suddenly the Industrial Revolution stemming from
Britain was to transform the whole human environment
at breakneck speed. Each generation from then on had
to wrestle with entirely new and unfamiliar problems.
Sources of power and the means of using it succeeded
each other at an ever-increasing rate. From coal to nuclear energy, from the steam engine to the jet, from the

telegraph to television, from the 20-mile-per-hour steam train to the 600-mile-per-hour airplane or the 25,000-mile-per-hour rocket, new discoveries and inventions were put at man's disposal in bewildering profusion. Our scientific knowledge has been expanding in a geometrical progression, and the trend continues. There is still no sign of a letup, no evidence of our having reached a new plateau on which we can rest a while and be given time to sort out our thoughts. That might certainly make it easier to so adjust human society that individuals' lives would be enriched by the incredible inventiveness of the human mind and not merely confused, or possibly extinguished, by it. But that time has not yet come, and now in every country industrialization has confronted human beings with a radically new way of life.

It was, of course, unlikely in the extreme that any existing society would find immediate or speedy solutions to the problems posed, and it is hardly surprising that all societies exposed to these powerful revolutionary forces have made mistakes. One of the more unfortunate consequences of the new technology has been that mistakes have become increasingly expensive and dangerous. But perhaps we shall at least be able to claim that in the light of these considerations Western civilization has not acquitted itself too badly.

First, however, we must have a look at the performance of other societies which have been confronted with the same phenomena. For convenience I shall take the Toynbee categories and cast an eye over those civilizations which he regards as still alive although in various stages of disrepair. The Far Eastern civilization, in the form it had taken in China or in Japan at the onset of the industrial age, has to all intents and purposes disintegrated. Some of the social and religious characteristics, of course, remain, but as a coherent whole, cementing together society in all its varied manifestations, Far Eastern civilization is practically unrecognizable. China has embraced Communism, which, I have suggested, is the antithesis of Western civilization, while Japan after a series of violent psychological shocks following upon the abandonment of her feudal isolationism in 1854, seems to have opted for a decidedly Western-oriented solution.

The Hindu civilization, already in decline, particularly since falling under European domination, appears to be unable to make any unique contribution to solving the problems of the industrial era. In certain respects it possesses religious and social characteristics which clash directly with the aspirations of its people to become part of a modern industrial state. The rigid caste system is one example. Another example is the attitude toward the sanctity of living creatures, and indeed toward life in all its forms, which has been an appalling handicap to more efficient agriculture and which has contributed to the population explosion, thus nullifying much of the gain brought about by increased national production.

I would add the following as a footnote to what I have said about Far Eastern and Hindu society. Anyone who has felt that the Western world no longer provides an ideal or spiritual faith which gives meaning to our lives and who entertains the hope that we might find refreshment in the East would do well to read Arthur Koestler's book *The Lotus and the Robot.* His attempt to find a stimulating spiritual spring in Hindu mysticism or in Buddhism is profoundly discouraging.

Next on our list come the Iranic and Arabic branches of the Islamic civilization, and although there is evidence of considerable vigor still in the field of religion, generally speaking, in the economic and even in the social field it has taken on a pronounced Western coloration. An example of the latter is the growth of equal rights and status for women and the related increase in the practice of monogamy among the more educated sections of the population.

Finally, the Eastern Orthodox Christian civilization, originally inspired by Constantinople, is now either in pawn to Communist regimes or has become identified with the mainstream of Western Christian civilization. Thus, we are led to the conclusion that the only serious competitor to our society is the Communist society, which to my mind has all the attributes of a separate civilization, although Professor Toynbee has resolutely refused to grant it such a status. He prefers to regard it as the abnormal offspring, or sport, of the Western and Eastern Orthodox civilizations. I will not pursue this partly semantic argument and will use the term "Communist civilization" freely, if perhaps inaccurately according to the purists. Whatever we call it, there is no doubt that we need to examine most carefully the performance of this form of society in dealing with our modern industrial and scientific environment.

Marxist-Leninism makes the claim that it is the first scientific political philosophy. This is both a strength and a weakness—a strength because it strikes a modern note and might be presumed to provide a more relevant answer to the problems of the age than any more ancient philosophy and a weakness because it conjures up an image of infallibility which it has found very hard to sustain in practice. Nothing is quite so deflating as to make an infallible prediction which is proved wrong. But its chief characteristic is that it exalts the collective over the individual, the state over man. Although there is much talk about the "dictatorship of the proletariat," a phrase which seems to have some democratic overtones and which is to be followed in the distant future by the "withering away of the state," in practice it means government by an elite minority whose members cannot be replaced individually or as a whole by the popular will and which has made itself self-perpetuating. There is sometimes a struggle for power within the ruling gang, but the admired proletariat plays no part in the struggle and usually has no knowledge of what is happening until it is all over. The most recent example was the enforced retirement of Khrushchev, but precisely the same thing had happened when Stalin replaced Lenin, when Malenkov replaced Stalin, and when Khrushchev himself replaced Malenkov.

This Marxist-Leninist priesthood makes the assumption that the vast majority of men and women are not competent or intelligent enough to run their own lives successfully and are therefore likely to be better off if the state arranges their priorities for them. Freedom from want is really the only freedom worth having, and for most of mankind individual freedom of choice puts upon them a burden they do not wish to bear. It is an avowedly materialist creed which claims that man does live by bread alone and that appeals to the spiritual side of man, apart from being unscientific, only create confusion in the mind and anarchy in the body politic. I know of no more penetrating analysis of this attitude of mind than the one that appears in the long parable of the Grand Inquisitor in Dostoevski's *The Brothers Karamazov.* You will remember how the Grand Inquisitor had come to the conclusion that the perpetual cry of mankind was "Make us your slaves but feed us."

This is all very repugnant to the liberal tradition of Western civilization, but we ought not to underrate the attractions of such a philosophy for millions of people who are utterly bewildered by the complications of modern life. They are tempted to say to themselves, "How am I expected to know and vote about the monetary and fiscal policy of the government, or about policy in South East Asia, or the size and content of the nuclear research program? I am ignorant of these matters. Let someone else take care of them so long as I am provided with a decent house, enough food and clothing for myself and my family, a steady job, and an old-age pension." To such people a totalitarian form of government has an appeal, and this to some extent accounts not only for the widespread acceptance of Communism but also for Hitler's popularity with a German people who were in despair about the conditions of life around them. Nor should we forget that at the time when Communism was making most of its intellectual converts in the Western world, in the 1930s, the system there seemed to be incapable of providing the elementary requirements demanded by my imaginary bewildered citizen. It appeared to be a system headed for the rocks, and a desire to embark on a different ship of state was not in the circumstances altogether a wild or fantastic one.

Finally, for a generation in which quite a number of people who found it difficult to reconcile religious beliefs with the new scientific knowledge, Communism offered an alternative ideal and a new cause to live and fight for. Anyone who had lost his faith in Christianity or other religion clearly no longer believed that every man or woman possessed a divine spark or soul which made his individuality of supreme value. If man were no more than a highly efficient animal, then the dream of a Communist society was not on the face of it an ignoble one. The trouble was that in practice many aspects of the dream became a nightmare.

In the first Communist state, established in Russia, millions died through the forced collectivization of the farms dictated by Marxist dogma. Political opponents were ruthlessly liquidated even when they were the most revered comrades who had given their whole lives to the establishment of Communism in the Soviet Union. Vast concentration camps swarmed with political prisoners, and no man was safe from the secret police. The hideous face of Communism in practice was for long hidden or at least veiled from the outside world, and right up to the death of Stalin the faithful Marxist disciple refused to believe the reality.

After Khrushchev came to power, it was at last revealed that the excesses resulting from the unbridled operation of such a system had in the end shocked even the rulers in the Kremlin. Reforms were instituted which mitigated the harshness of the regime, and much of the machinery of terror was dismantled. This liberalization spread to other Communist countries in Eastern Europe, with uncomfortable results for the regimes in Poland and still more in Hungary. All this was watched with extreme distaste by the Communist leaders in Peking, and Khrushchev was branded as a "revisionist"—as indeed he was.

It would be fair to say, however, that some of the more revolting features of Marxist society have been at any rate temporarily removed in the Soviet Union, and to this extent some of the attractions of the philosophy on which it is built can again exert their pull on the underprivileged or disenchanted around the world.

Turning from what one might call the philosophical aspects of Communism, let us look for a moment at its performance in the economic and political field. By centralized planning and the laying down of rigid priorities coupled with the strictest regimentation of labor, the Soviet Union managed to achieve a very rapid expansion of its industrial power. Savings to provide for the necessary capital investment were squeezed out of the workers with a ruthlessness that made the worst excesses of the capitalist system look positively benevolent. But the job was done and a formidable base of heavy industry established, and there is no doubt that during this early stage in the economic development of the Soviet Union a high rate of increase in the gross national product was achieved, certainly a higher rate than was being achieved in Western countries at the same date. Only agriculture remained a most conspicuous laggard.

Russia was still in this relatively simple and primitive stage of industrial growth when World War II broke out. In that war her richest provinces were overrun and subjected to wholesale destruction, so that in the first decade after 1945 she found herself back again in much the same early stage of growth, and again her expansion was at a high rate. It is therefore only in recent years that the Soviet Union has had to face the problems that confront an industrial society when it has become more affluent, more complex, and more sophisticated. At this stage, which the United States and other Western countries had long ago reached, priorities became much less easy for the planners to determine, the absence of an effective price mechanism confused the whole picture, and high rates of increase in production were harder to come by.

Under these conditions the Soviet economy has been showing many signs of strain, and in the 1960s industrial expansion has slowed considerably, often falling below that achieved in Western countries. This is a most significant development, and there is little evidence that the Russians have found satisfactory solutions to the problems that have arisen. In particular, the agricultural industry is a conspicuous and embarrassing straggler which is holding back the whole convoy. Although in proportion to its population Russia has vast tracts of fertile farm land which if efficiently cultivated ought to produce huge surpluses for export, she has in fact had to dig deeply into her gold reserves more than once in order to buy grain from abroad to feed her people and livestock.

But in industry generally it is clear that all has not been well for some time. Plans for decentralization and then for centralization succeed each other with bewildering rapidity, and the Soviet press is full of denunciations of inefficiency and corruption. One intriguing indicator of the state of affairs could be seen in the reintroduction of the death penalty for economic crimes. In mid-1963, when I last had a count made of the number of executions that had been reported, the total was already about 200. This is indeed an astonishing phenomena. Here we have the new model society which had once decreed the abolition of the death penalty and had been the darling of those who thought themselves progressive, executing people for graft and such crimes, a practice that has long since been considered barbarous in the Western world. Surely no government, however indifferent to human life, would impose such penalties unless compelled to do so to stop a widespread and crippling mischief in the economic life of the country.

In spite of the numerous signs of strain in the Soviet economy, showing that even a supposedly scientific theory of government is fallible, we ought not to underestimate its strength. By adherence to strict priorities, it can still nourish the sinews of power at the expense of the consumer. Rockets for space and defense, nuclear weapons, submarines, and tanks are thus all produced in great profusion, while automobiles remain as rare as they were in America fifty years ago and housing lags far behind the level attained in Western countries of similar wealth. Perhaps above all we should note that the Soviet's educational system has been turning out scientists, engineers, and technicians at a faster rate in proportion to the population than any other country, and this trend is bound to make an important contribution to its economic strength in the future.

On the external political front, Communism still retains an attraction for poor and underdeveloped countries which are struggling desperately to take off into the industrial era. The Soviet Union's history of development from a backward, mainly agrarian society into an industrial giant in little more than a generation seems to offer an example with greater affinity to the predicament they find themselves in than the history of the much earlier development of Britain and America. Then, Communism offers a creed, which, at any rate in theory, is anticolonial and nonracial; and while it is true that the advantages the Communist can achieve from the anti-colonialist cry have diminished with the rapid disappearance of colonialism, their more recent emphasis on economic or neocolonialism can still strike a responsive chord among people who feel they are exploited.

Generally speaking, however, the appeal of Marxism in the non-Communist world and particularly in Western society has been blunted by the far greater success that has attended the management by the West of both its economic and its political affairs. Higher living standards, low unemployment, and expanding social security with an insignificant surrender of personal freedom— these do not provide a fertile soil for the seed of Marxism. Then again, the appeal of a universal philosophy which claimed to eliminate the stresses and contradictions that plagued older forms of human society is looking more than a little flyblown with the rise of nationalism in the former Soviet satellites of Eastern Europe and the much more serious split that has grown even wider and deeper between Russia and China. The claim that a theory which produces quite different answers in Moscow and Peking is scientific can be met only with derision.

For the sake of brevity I have concentrated my examination on the Soviet Union, which among Communist societies is the most powerful, the longest established, and the most advanced. One could, of course, trace parallel developments in the other Communist countries. China is still in the earliest stage of her revolution, and with fewer natural resources and a much larger burden of population than Russia her performance in the agricultural field will be of far greater importance. The failure so far of all Communist countries to develop a vigorous agriculture must for China be a most discouraging omen. The countries of Eastern Europe vary considerably in the degree of industrialization they have achieved. Eastern Germany is one of the more advanced, but it is interesting to note that the establishment of a so-called "workers' paradise" in that territory necessitated, to paraphrase Winston Churchill, the building of a prodigious wall coupled with barbed-wire entanglements to prevent the cherubim and seraphim from getting out.

Let me try and sum up the record of Communist civilization so far. In the economic field, in spite of remarkable early progress which it would be foolish to deny, it now seems to be floundering. Indeed, it is difficult to pinpoint areas in which it is being more successful than Western civilization in solving the problems of a modern industrial society and easy to find those in which it is being less successful. In particular, it seems far less capable of meeting the real desires of the consumer. Politically, it still poses a real challenge to us. It has retained all the territorial gains it made as a result of the war and its aftermath and has achieved two more minor but significant expansions in North Viet Nam and in Cuba. Nationalism has, however, been steadily eroding the monolithic structure which seemed so formidable at the time of Stalin's death, and the coming into existence of two rival fountainheads, both claiming to disseminate the infallible doctrines of Marxism but contradicting each other, has inevitably weakened the political thrust of Communism. Militarily, in spite of superhuman efforts, the Soviet Union failed to achieve superiority over the West which would have given her a trump card in international affairs. Her failure in this respect was made clear to the world when she had to climb down after the confrontation with the United States over Cuba in October, 1962. Socially, there is no evidence that in Communist societies human beings achieve a greater sense of fulfillment or sense of harmony with their environment than in Western societies—rather the reverse.

In the arts, freedom of expression remains minimal, and it is therefore not surprising to find that artistic expression is less imaginative and more conservative than in almost any other existing society. Whenever a whiff of freedom has been granted, the results have been so intoxicating that there has been an immediate danger of the authorities' losing control. This was true of the liberalization in the literary field in Russia. It was even more apparent following the overthrow of Stalinism in Poland and was to be seen in its most extreme form in Hungary in 1956. These examples strongly suggest that many of the basic intellectual needs of men and women are not being satisfied in Communist society.

I began this chapter by saying that since all human institutions are imperfect, we can judge Western civilization only in relation to the performance of other existing civilizations and to the problems posed by our environment. I have suggested that with the possible exception of Communist civilization we have no serious competitors and that in the case of this our chief rival, there are flaws and weaknesses as great as or greater than those to which we ourselves are heir.

As for our performance in relation to the unprecedented environment we find ourselves in, I have tried to indicate that, while there is still the danger of a relapse in many fields, we have learned from previous mistakes and have been making a fairly good job of solving problems that originally baffled us. Internecine warfare, which had ravaged Western civilization in the first half of this century, seemed unlikely to recur, and since this type of warfare has been by far the commonest cause for the decline of civilizations in the past, this is a most encouraging development. The idolization of the parochial sovereign state, which had so enormously increased the bitterness and the destructiveness of these wars, seemed to be giving way to a spirit of unity and cooperation that gave new strength and hope to the West. Here, however, there are signs of backsliding. Socially, over the last century, much had been done, from the abolition of slavery, through the development of trade unions, which brought a better balance between the rights of labor and the rights of property, and through a variety of adjustments to the economic machine to create satisfactory living conditions for the mass of our peoples. Great progress had been achieved in expanding educational opportunities, thus opening up an intellectual treasure house for all which had previously been the privileged possession of the few.

Above all, our whole society has been leavened by the idea of liberty under law, rooted in our religious tradition, which combines responsibility toward society and our fellow men with encouragement to the individual to explore the furthermost frontiers of the mind as well as those of the physical universe. Herein I believe lies our greatest strength. It seems to me highly improbable that men who are blinkered and dragooned by the society in which they live can hope to match the ability of free men to adapt themselves to a rapidly changing environment.

In this context one doubt haunts me. If it is true that many of the values we hold most dear in our society have their roots in religious beliefs, can we be sure that they will survive in a spiritual vacuum? Are we perhaps living on religious capital which if not replenished by renewed faith will melt away and be replaced by a purely materialistic and opportunist attitude to human affairs? We must hope that the ecumenical movement and the new vitality displayed in the Roman Catholic and other churches heralds the arrival of reinforcements for our society on the spiritual front.

Finally, we must bear in mind that even though we may have right on our side, we can yet be overwhelmed by might. Unfortunately, history furnishes us with all too many examples of great civilizations going down before the forces of barbarism because of the latter's greater numbers or greater military power. For the time being, there is no need for Western civilization to fear such an outcome if it retains its unity and keeps up its military guard. The Western countries contain the most numerous force of skilled manpower in the world, they produce over two-thirds of the world's steel and electricity, and they control four-fifths of its oil supplies; and one could give numerous other examples to show that it will not fail through lack of resources. Nevertheless, it could still fail as a result of foolish policies, and I shall try next to indicate what policies I think it needs to pursue to guard against such failure and to insure that Western civilization, improved and matured, extends its benefits to all mankind.

THREE

What Needs to Be Done

WE HAVE NOTED that civilizations decline, or collapse
entirely, for a whole variety of reasons. The chief causes
have been, first, internal decay frequently manifesting
itself in the form of internecine warfare, second, exposure to a superior form of society, third, stagnation in
the military arts leading to a critical inferiority, and,
fourth, some inherent physical inferiority such as a lack
of resources or of numbers. The first and second of these
causes are closely related, as are the third and fourth.

I have also suggested that in certain of its aspects the
history of Western civilization gives us no absolute
assurance that it will survive and flourish in the future.
On the other hand, there is no law of historical determin-
ism, and human civilizations are not comparable to living
organisms. They have no inevitable life cycle of birth,
growth, virile youth, comfortable middle-age, senility,
and death as has been suggested by Paul Valéry and Os-
wald Spengler. The causes of the rise and decline of
civilizations are to an overwhelming degree traceable to
the ideas and the actions of men who are continually

being replaced in a society as generation succeeds generation. In other words, except in the case of inherent physical inferiority, the rise and the decline are directly attributable to the making of right decisions or of wrong decisions by a large number of individual human beings.

In the case that we are examining, namely, Western civilization, physical inferiority is not a factor. The material resources, whether in raw materials or in manufacturing skills, are available to the West in abundance. In the sinews of power we command a substantial superiority. In the case of the comparative size of populations, it is true that if we take only those countries which are fully committed on the side of Communism and allow a figure of 650 million for China, which may well be too high, we obtain a total of about 950 million, while for countries fully committed on the Western side the total is only about 600 million. The disparity is not significant, however, and we can feel confident that we are not in danger of being overwhelmed by sheer numbers.

Of the four chief causes of decline we can therefore say that with one the danger does not arise for us at present, and in the case of the other three we are not automatically doomed by an inexorable law of nature. The choice is in our own hands. Either we can do what is necessary to preserve and improve upon our civilization, or we can fail to do what is necessary and court decay if not disaster.

Let us then take the three remaining categories which are susceptible to our own control and try to see where our weaknesses lie and what we can do to eradicate them.

First let us look at the military sphere, which in many ways is the easiest to assess. Here we find that, so far as Western society is concerned, there has been no stagnation in the military arts. It is true that for one brief period after 1945 the whole of Western Europe was put in jeopardy by a very rapid demobilization of conventional forces on the part of the principal free world victors, the United States and Britain, while the Soviet Union retained forces which outnumbered ours by three to one. At the time, however, the American monopoly of nuclear weapons and a rapid reappraisal of the situation following the rape of Czechoslovakia and the Berlin blockade averted a major tragedy, and technically the West has retained its general superiority over its principal rival in the military field as well as over all other living civilizations. For this fact we owe a tremendous debt of gratitude to the American people and to successive United States governments. Owing to their farsightedness and to a very heavy expenditure of money and technical skill, the West is equal or superior to the Communists in nuclear power, in missile technology, and in military mobility. We can therefore claim that the Western countries have the capability and until now have had the will to keep up their military guard. How we may best deploy and control our combined military resources is more a political question, and I will deal with some aspects of it when I discuss the internal structure of Western society. But before I come to this, I shall digress in order to discuss briefly a matter which at least deserves a mention.

I am referring here to the question that any intelligent person must ask himself from time to time—whether human civilizations of any sort or kind are going to survive. The question is clearly not unimportant, and if the answer were to be in the negative, I would now be wasting not only your time but mine. Seriously, though, any country which has acquired advanced technical knowledge about atomic weapons and whose government possesses a significant nuclear potential has had to examine seriously the consequences of using such weapons. In theory it is possible so to control their use that some semblance of human society would survive, but no one who has taken a hard look at the problem can feel sure that this would be the case in practice. If the nuclear exchange did get out of control and the indiscriminate bombardment of population centers did take place, then it is entirely possible that all semblance of human civilization on this planet would be obliterated. Whether life of any sort could long be supported is questionable, and even if it could, we can be sure that the living would envy the dead. These facts must lead us to only one conclusion, that war must be eliminated as a method of trying to settle disputes between nations. Small wars as well as big wars, conventional wars as well as nuclear wars, for small wars may escalate so that great powers become involved on both sides, and even if agreement could now be reached to eliminate all nuclear weapons, which is most unlikely, a conventional war between the great powers would become a nuclear one as each side raced to remanufacture its atomic weapons, since the knowledge of how to make such weapons cannot now be eliminated.

Having said that war must cease to be an arbiter in disputes between nations, one is uncomfortably aware of the fact that it has plagued human society since the dawn of history and that what we are demanding is a change in human behavior which will defy all precedents. Above all, it means abandoning certain attitudes of mind which belong to the pre-atomic era but nevertheless remain embedded in the thoughts of us who belong to an older generation and are resown in the minds of younger generations as they learn the history of their nation. Retaining these attitudes is inevitable but not dangerous if they are supplemented by a true understanding of the present scientific position which makes a pre-atomic attitude to war an absurdity. As they acquire real knowledge, I believe that even the Peking government will stop talking puerile nonsense about atomic war and put more real science into their thinking and less sham science into their political philosophy.

The peaceful settlement of disputes is absolutely necessary to preserve any human civilization, and that is why I am not one of those that decries the United Nations. Rather I grieve at its present weakness and am angered by those who scoff at it and seek to diminish its role. It is an organization which needs improvement and reform, but the major improvement needed is in the performance of the individual governments that make up its membership. All this, however, is a different and in some ways a wider topic, and having touched on it, I shall simply add that this book is based on the hypothesis that human civilizations will continue to exist and to compete with each other. I am by no means allergic to the phrase "peaceful coexistence" even if it was coined by the Communists. I just wish that those who talk about it so much would genuinely practice it.

To return then to my main theme, I had concluded that Western civilization did not seem to be threatened by stagnation or inferiority in the military arts, and I was about to examine the evidence with regard to internal decay. I think it will be more convenient if I divide this examination into two parts. First there are the problems of human relations within the nation states, or what one might call the domestic policies of these states, and second there are the problems associated with relations among the states which make up Western civilization.

As regards domestic policies, if we are to retain the belief of men and women that ours is a superior form of society to any of its rivals, then we shall have to demonstrate that it more nearly meets human needs and human desires than they do. Having proclaimed ourselves champions of the individual and of his right to justice and freedom, we have to ask ourselves whether our national societies live up to these high aspirations. Does the rule of law genuinely prevail throughout the land? Is justice truly impartial in the case of every citizen from the highest to the lowest? Do we provide generously enough for the casualties in our society, for the weak, for the sick, and for the old? Are we conducting our economic affairs in such a way as to secure maximum exployment and the necessary resources for the development of the good life? Are we creating an environment in our great cities, where the vast majority of our populations are now condemned to live, which can give to human beings dignity and a feeling of physical and spiritual contentment? Our civilization will be judged by these criteria and many others, but I do not intend to discuss these matters in detail, because I am very well aware that I would very soon find myself in the turbulent waters and the uncertain currents of United States domestic politics. I was Ambassador in Washington a sufficiently short time ago to remember the sad fate of my predecessor, Lord Sackville, who got himself involved in an American election and was rapidly recalled to London. I am, however, prepared to say this. All of us, from whatever country we come, are well aware of blemishes within our societies. The vast majority of them require and are susceptible to national remedies. It is our duty as responsible citizens to see these remedies applied, for we can be sure that the human race is always watching to see whether we in practice live up to the high ideals that we preach.

We must be equally concerned about, and I am certainly freer to talk about, relations among the nations that constitute the central body of Western civilization. Earlier I have said that as a result of the industrial and scientific revolution of the nineteenth century the sovereign nation-state was rapidly becoming an anachronism. The nation still had an indispensable part to play in the scheme of things, but it was no longer complete and sufficient in itself, nor could it act solely in its own self-interest and ignore the interests of others without dire consequences and eventually intolerable friction. To be precise, the individual nation is an incomplete and inadequate framework for modern society in two main spheres—the economic sphere and the politico-military sphere. In both of these there is a need to put relations between states on a different footing from that which existed during the first four decades of this century, and what worries me is that this need was much more widely accepted in the late 1940s and in the 1950s than it has been in the last five years.

As we have seen, the West made a good start after the war. In the economic field the International Monetary Fund brought confidence and order to the currency and exchange structure of the non-Communist world. The General Agreement on Tariffs and Trade performed a similar task for world trade. The World Bank promoted foreign investment and development, and in Europe the Organization for European Economic Co-operation co-ordinated the plans for the reconstruction of a war-stricken continent with American finance. In the political and defense field a new type of integrated alliance, the North Atlantic Treaty Organization, was created and within Western Europe a trend towards an even higher degree of integration made steady progress from the establishment of the Coal and Steel Community to the setting-up of the European Economic Community with the avowed objective of developing into a political community. The Council of Europe and the Western European Union were also formed with good intentions but have made no significant contribution to unity since their birth. Finally, the European Free Trade Association has helped to provide an economic haven for those excluded from the Common Market.

Up to 1961 we had been moving slowly but surely along the right road, and in that year Britain made what was for her an historic decision to seek full membership of the EEC and so to cast her lot irrevocably and forever with her continental neighbors in Europe. She had taken a long time, some would say too long, to make up her mind, but there were good explanations, if not good excuses, for her previous indecision. For centuries she had tried to avoid being too closely entangled on the Continent. She had come victorious through two great wars and had avoided the physical and psychological damage resulting from foreign occupation. She was responsible for a family of nations established in every ocean and on every continent. It was hard for the British people, in these circumstances, to understand why they needed to abandon traditional policies that, on the face of it, had served them fairly well in the past. At last Britain had overcome her hesitation, and in the spirit of my mother's family motto, *sero sed serio*—"late but in earnest," she sought to join the European caravan.

The following summer, while negotiations for our entry to the Common Market, which it was hoped would also unlock the door for the other members of EFTA, were progressing, President Kennedy made his celebrated speech in Philadelphia on Independence Day, proclaiming America's desire to see the growth of interdependence among the nations of the West, culminating in an, as he put it, "a concrete Atlantic Partnership . . . between the new union now emerging in Europe and the old American Union founded here 175 years ago." "Let the world know [this] is our goal," he added, and millions then hoped and prayed it was. I was certainly among them. But is it still our goal today? One is bound to have grave doubts. Much has gone wrong since we reached that highwater mark of unity and common purpose in July, 1962. Six months later Britain was excluded from the Common Market against the wishes of five out of its six members. The doctrine was promulgated that a country desiring close ties with the United States was not genuinely European, that integration within the North Atlantic Alliance had served a fleeting purpose but ought to be dismantled now that the nations of Europe had recovered from the war. Are we not once again hearing the Sirens' voices calling us back to the glorification of the nation state? Unlike Odysseus' comrades, we cannot stop up our ears against those voices, but we do not have to be bewitched by them. All that we had jointly achieved since the end of the war was not just a temporary diversion while the old main road was being repaired, it was a start on the construction of a new type of highway suited to the age we live in. We must not allow work on it to be held up much longer.

I now come to concrete cases where improvement seems clearly needed, and the first of these that I want to deal with comes under the broad heading of international liquidity. We all understand reasonably well that if in our own countries we wish to have an expanding economy, we must have machinery for expanding the supply of money and credit. In the old days, when this machinery was of a rudimentary kind, gold played a predominant part, and the purely fortuitous discovery of gold, as in California in 1849, could lead to an economic boom, and the falling-off of supplies of the metal could lead to a slump. This was not a particularly rational or sensible way of regulating the supply of money, although variations in the price of gold gave it some flexibility, and gradually more sophisticated means of providing for an expanding credit base for the economy were devised.

We have not managed nearly so well in the field of international monetary policy. In broad terms, it has been calculated that in order to cope with the demand generated by the rising level of world trade an increase in the money supply of about $3 billion per annum is required. So long, however, as most countries insist that in-

ternational currencies must be immediately convertible
into gold, the only effective increase to the money supply comes from the flow of newly mined gold into offi-
cial reserves, but this flow is probably no more than $1
billion per annum. We can thus see that unless we create
a system for the regular and substantial expansion of the
supply of money and credit there is bound to be a con-
stant tendency for world trade to slacken off and for de-
flation to set in, starting with a general weakening in
commodity prices. The true situation has been masked in
recent years because both the international currencies,
the dollar and the pound, have been pumping money
into the system out of their own reserves. But this practice cannot go on forever or even for very much longer,
and now, more than twenty years after Bretton Woods,
the time has come to reform the International Monetary
Fund in such a way that it becomes in effect a central
bank for the free world.

I do not wish to get involved in the technicalities, but
two things are clear. The first is that if it is impossible to
increase the price of gold, partly for American constitu-
tional reasons, then the Fund must have the power to
create and to expand the supply of some international re-
serve unit of money. The second is that if this is to be
done, the Fund will to some extent require that member
countries merge their sovereignty in this specific field.
No doubt there will be incorporated a system of
weighted voting, and I see no good reason that all coun-

seek membership thus finding again in a larger grouping a natural unity of purpose with the country of which she was formerly a reluctant part.

At this stage the United States Trade Expansion Act of 1962 would once more achieve its full significance, for you will recall that it contained provisions which, had we become members of the Common Market, would have given the President powers to negotiate the reduction of tariffs to zero over a wide range of industrial goods. If implemented this would in effect have meant the creation of a free-trade area in industrial products throughout the North Atlantic community. When the way ahead is again clear, I hope it will be possible for the United States Congress to renew the mandate given to the President to eliminate barriers to trade between like-minded nations, for then together with a soundly based international monetary structure we shall have the framework within which we can tackle some of the major problems that confront the world—aid to the underdeveloped countries, greater stability for commodity prices, and agricultural surpluses. These problems are related and require ever more urgent attention if they are to be prevented from becoming a source of intolerable friction between nations within the Western community and still more between the have and have-not nations outside that community.

Something can be and, of course, is being done to wrestle with these problems while the West remains in its present state of disorder, but it is hard to see how our

tries should not be prepared for this degree of i
pendence. It will redound to their general well-be

The second case I want to deal with is intern
trade, and here there is not too much that the I
States can do to help until we in Europe have p
house in order. It is impossible to carry on a di
with an entity that has no voice because one of its
bers refuses to speak to the others. This means no
that progress is halted within the Common Mark
that progress toward a general reduction in trade
riers in the so-called "Kennedy round" of GATT
tiations is also at a standstill. The deadlock withi
EEC therefore affects us all, but we must not be to
patient, for if a resumption of activity at the present
can be purchased only by an abandonment of the
principles and concept of the Rome Treaty, then
would be far too high a price to pay. It would be a n
triumph for old-fashioned nationalism and a breec
faith with those who, deeply conscious of the vast s
human misery such nationalism has caused, have so
to build a better Europe. The EEC must regain its
mentum, and then I hope the day will not be far di
when Britain joins as a full member, not grudgingly
joyously and inspired by the challenge of helping
construct one of the finest edifices of Western civi
tion. If Britain joins, her partners in the EFTA
either themselves become full members or assoc
members of the EEC. The Republic of Ireland will

full potential can be brought to bear until our efforts are far more closely integrated and we have achieved a greater unity of purpose and a fairer sharing of burdens. Particularly in the last few years we seem to have become weary of well-doing over aid to the poorer nations —and here I am not concerned with military aid. George Woods wrote not long ago that "at a growth rate of 5 percent, the underdeveloped countries would, seventy-five years from now, reach the same average income a head as the countries of Western Europe were enjoying in 1960." But in the majority of cases the poorer nations are achieving nothing like that growth rate. In many it is no more than 1 percent. They are desperately short of capital for investment and are beset by many other difficulties. Too often prices for their commodities have fallen in such a way as to wipe out entirely the value of foreign aid received, and now the cost of servicing the loans they have been granted is absorbing 40 percent of the new help they are receiving. Many of them have to import food for their exploding populations from industrialized countries which are holding back agricultural production to avoid being choked by surpluses.

Under these conditions it is sad to see Britain and the United States ceasing to expand their foreign aid, partly for balance-of-payment reasons. It is certainly not because the amount of foreign aid they have been giving has reduced their standard of living. Indeed, in 1964, when the United States held its foreign aid at about the previous year's figure, its own gross national product increased by $40 billion. Here again we are in a sphere where Western society will be measured against its professed principles and will have to meet competition on an increasing scale from Communist countries. The task before us is one that cannot be effectively accomplished except through a joint enterprise based upon the massive strength of a single financial and trading unit.

I come now to the final case where I believe we need to improve existing arrangements or devise new ones if the West is to guard against internal decay. It embraces the whole complex of political relationships and defense and raises the question what is to be the structure of the "concrete Atlantic Partnership" of which President Kennedy spoke. I see little value in designing blueprints for the distant future which pay too little attention to what might be possible in the next stage ahead of us. For this reason I believe it to be quite useless to hanker after plans for drawing together Eastern and Western Europe and worse still to delay certain moves in the West, for fear it might make the implementation of such plans even less conceivable than they are already. The idea of a united Europe stretching from the Atlantic to the Eastern border of Poland, let alone the Urals, is a chimera which can only serve to divert us from the real task before us, which is to construct a united Western Europe—a task that is entirely feasible. Until this is done, the relation between the United States and individual countries in Europe will be uneasy and unsatisfactory to both parties.

I do not know of any country which has tried harder

to take into account the views of its allies than the United States, but when all these views vary and are even contradictory, what is the United States to do? To do nothing is rarely wise, but to act is usually to court displeasure in some allied capital. It is often said that Europe now restored in strength and self-confidence should be given a greater say in the conduct of affairs in the Western alliance, but to whom is America to listen—to France, to Germany, to Italy, or to Britain? She cannot please them all unless on important issues they have a common approach, while so long as they speak as individuals, the inequality in strength, in influence, and in the burden they carry compared with the United States places them in an unsatisfactory relationship and one that is unsatisfactory on both sides. A united Europe with Britain participating would constitute an entity whose size and power would be broadly comparable to that of the older union on the Western side of the Atlantic, and it would then be possible to set up one or more joint commissions on which two equal partners would be represented. It might be argued that this means that individual European governments would be surrendering what is sometimes called "an independent foreign policy," but these are no more than words to mystify the millions. No nation can now have a truly independent foreign policy, and smaller nations which try to pretend they can finish up independent no doubt but with no influence whatever over the course of world events.

I do not deny that there is a danger that as the coming

into being of a united Europe would make it less dependent on the United States, this new great power might be tempted to pursue policies conceived to be in its own interest but contrary to the interest of its trans-Atlantic partner. Certainly a Third Force of this kind could generate centrifugal forces within Western civilization, but the central core of my argument throughout this book has been that in reality we share common interests and that on the most vitally important issues we aim at common objectives. If there is any danger of the two ends of the dumbbell flying apart, then I see all the more reason for establishing institutions which will tie them firmly together.

In no sphere are the interests of the two sides of the Atlantic more closely bound to each other than in that of defense. With megaton war-heads carried on missiles with a range of 8,000 miles, defense policies can have validity only if they are conceived on a global scale. This means that no country can have self-sufficient armed forces, and their defense efforts will be largely an expensive bluff and a fraud unless they are deliberately planned to contribute to an effective whole which can discharge the role of defending Western civilization. At the present time the United States and Britain are the only countries who carry military responsibilities both inside and outside the NATO area. I do not think it is practical politics to expect other members of the alliance to take over a share in our commitments elsewhere in the world, but I think they must take into account these heavy burdens in considering what contribution the United States and Britain can fairly be asked to undertake within the NATO area. Apart from this, over a great range of subjects from force levels and strategy to weapon development and arms manufacture, the West needs an even closer integration of its defense effort and the minimum unit that makes sense is an Atlantic one.

This above all is true in the nuclear field, but here we run into some special difficulties. Ever since the war and even today, the United States has owned and controlled an overwhelming proportion of the nuclear might of the West. This has led to tensions within the alliance and feelings in Europe that they cannot accept the principle of incineration without representation. Basically, the British and French nuclear programs have been designed to insure that some attention is paid to their views before nuclear decisions are taken. The United States on its side is naturally reluctant to have some other country trigger off a nuclear exchange which in its later stages will solely concern America and Russia. And finally we have the formidable problems posed by Germany's need to feel that she is not cast forever in the role of the provider of conventionally armed mercenaries for the defense of Western Europe but has some share of responsibility in the nuclear field. The Multilateral Force for nuclear weapons was designed as an answer to these problems on an Atlantic basis, and I still believe that some variation on this theme will prove the best solution in the long run. Some people in Europe are not yet convinced, however, that American and European interests will always run parallel, and they would like to hold open the option of transforming such a nuclear force into a purely European one at some future date.

I suppose it is conceivable that American policy in ten or twenty years might develop in such a way that Western Europe could no longer count upon United States help, although I do not think it likely myself, and in these circumstances a nuclear deterrent would become a necessity for a Europe lying in the shadow of the Soviet's military might. In the light of these feelings, I see little harm in holding open the option particularly as by building up the Atlantic links I have already mentioned we could insure that the eventuality of a split down the Atlantic never arose.

I have not attempted in so short a space to deal in detail with many of these problems of cooperation, and I have sought no more than to give examples of those matters where the interests of all Western society are mutual and where it would be greatly to our advantage to handle them jointly rather than separately or in competition with each other. If the argument is valid, then we can see the outline of the trans-Atlantic partnership which we need to construct and which will act as the indestructible framework for our Western civilization. First, a Western European community, of which Britain is a full member, with economic and political institutions which will provide unity of policy and purpose and which will possess an economic and industrial potential roughly equivalent to that of the United States. Second, a United States of America and Canada on the Western side of the Atlantic even more powerful and prosperous. And third, these two giant communities linked together by machinery which insures that in international monetary policy, in trade policy, in defense policy, and in political objectives, there is a far higher degree of harmonization than there is today. All will have to accept some merging of sovereignty if the whole is to function efficiently. I see no good reason that in this modern world any of us should shrink from this prospect, least of all the United States, whose very existence stands as a monument to the almost incredible benefits that flow from combining together in prescribed fields to perform a common task. Indeed, it will not be enough for the United States to urge a merging of sovereignty on others unless she is also prepared to set an example herself.

The goal of a real Atlantic Community seems to me a noble one. If we can achieve it, Western civilization will present to the entire world a society that is both materially and spiritually more satisfying to men and women than anything the doctrines of Karl Marx and his disciples can fashion. But if we aim at no such goal and allow ourselves to be dragged back slowly but surely into the jungle of competitive nationalism, then I see a bleak future for our civilization. Perhaps for a brief moment of history one country or another may bask in a temporary blaze of glory as by maneuvering among its fellow heirs to this civilization, it gains a fleeting advantage over them. But in reality the sun will be going down on a great age in the human story. The uncommitted world will look on with disgust. Marx will appear to have been right in his prophecies, and mankind may enter into a long night of enslavement under a ruthless, materialistic creed.

Index